Tom Tierney

Tom Tierney

The young Queen Victoria of England

The stylish Empress Eugénie of France

PLATE 1

Do not cut out white area
between arm and body.

1900
Dinner gown by Callot Sœurs

1900
Ball gown by Dœuillet

PLATE 15

Do not cut out white area
between arm and body.

1900
Promenade gown with dotted net trim by Drecoll

1900
Afternoon dress with heavy cotton lace trim
by Maison Rouff

PLATE 14

Do not cut out white area
between arm and body.

1884
Walking suit by Mme. Merlet Tarot

1888
Dinner gown by Gustave Janet

PLATE 13

1878
Princess gown of green crepe de chine by Worth

1885
Day dress for the Princess Beatrice's trousseau
by Redfern

PLATE 12

1873
Visiting toilette from *Harper's Bazar*
(taken from *La Mode Artistique*)

PLATE 11

Do not cut out white area
between arm and body.

1873
Evening toilette by Worth

PLATE 10

1867
Sportswear by Gilguin *fils*

1872
Dolly Varden walking suit (named after a character
in Dickens' *Barnaby Rudge*) from *Harper's Bazar*

PLATE 9

1864
"Peacock gown" designed by Worth
for the Princess de Sagan

PLATE 8

1860
Evening dress from the *Journal des Demoiselles*

PLATE 7

1858
Pelisse wrap from Gagelin

1858
Visiting suit from Golquin et Depain

PLATE 6

1856
Afternoon dress from Gagelin

1857
Riding attire (possibly by Creed)

PLATE 5

1845
Evening dress by Charles Frederick Worth

1847
A walking dress by Mrs. Wood
(a New York dressmaker and milliner)

PLATE 4

1836
Paris gown of mousseline by Mlle. Pierlot

1840
Afternoon dress in pale lavender silk by Camille

PLATE 3

1840
Victoria's wedding gown (possibly by John Redfern)
of white satin trimmed with bobbin lace

ca. 1854
Eugénie's court gown (possibly by Mme. Vignon)

PLATE 2